TOMMY'

£1

FABULOUS MUSIC LIMITED

Exclusive Distributors:
MUSIC SALES LIMITED
8/9 Frith Street,
London W1V 5TZ, England.
MUSIC SALES PTY LIMITED
120 Rothschild Avenue,
Rosebery, NSW 2018,
Australia.

Order No.AM937453
ISBN 0-7119-5805-X
This book © Copyright 1996 by Fabulous Music Limited
Visit the Music Sales' Internet Music Shop at
http://www.musicsales.co.uk

Music arranged by Roger Day
Music processed by Paul Ewers Music Design
Book design by Pearce Marchbank, Studio Twenty
Quarked by Ben May

Printed in the United Kingdom by
Redwood Books Limited, Trowbridge, Wiltshire.

YOUR GUARANTEE OF QUALITY
As publishers, we strive to produce every book to the highest commercial
standards. The music has been freshly engraved
and the book has been carefully designed to minimise awkward page turns and
to make playing from it a real pleasure. Particular care has been given to
specifying acid-free, neutral-sized paper made from pulps which have not
been elemental chlorine bleached.
This pulp is from farmed sustainable forests and was produced
with special regard for the environment. Throughout, the printing
and binding have been planned to ensure a sturdy, attractive publication
which should give years of enjoyment.
If your copy fails to meet our high standards,
please inform us and we will gladly replace it.

Music Sales' complete catalogue describes thousands of
titles and is available in full colour sections by subject, direct from
Music Sales Limited. Please state your areas of interest
and send a cheque/postal order for £1.50 for postage to:
Music Sales Limited, Newmarket Road,
Bury St. Edmunds, Suffolk IP33 3YB.

OVERTURE

WORDS & MUSIC BY PETER TOWNSHEND

Spoken: The union of husband and wife in heart, body and mind is intended by God for their mutual joy;
for the procreation of children and their nurture in the knowledge and love of the Lord.

for the help and comfort given one another in prosperity and adversity;
Therefore, marriage is not to be entered into unadvisedly or lightly, but reverently deliberately,

and when it is God's will,
and in accordance with the purpose for which it was instituted by God.

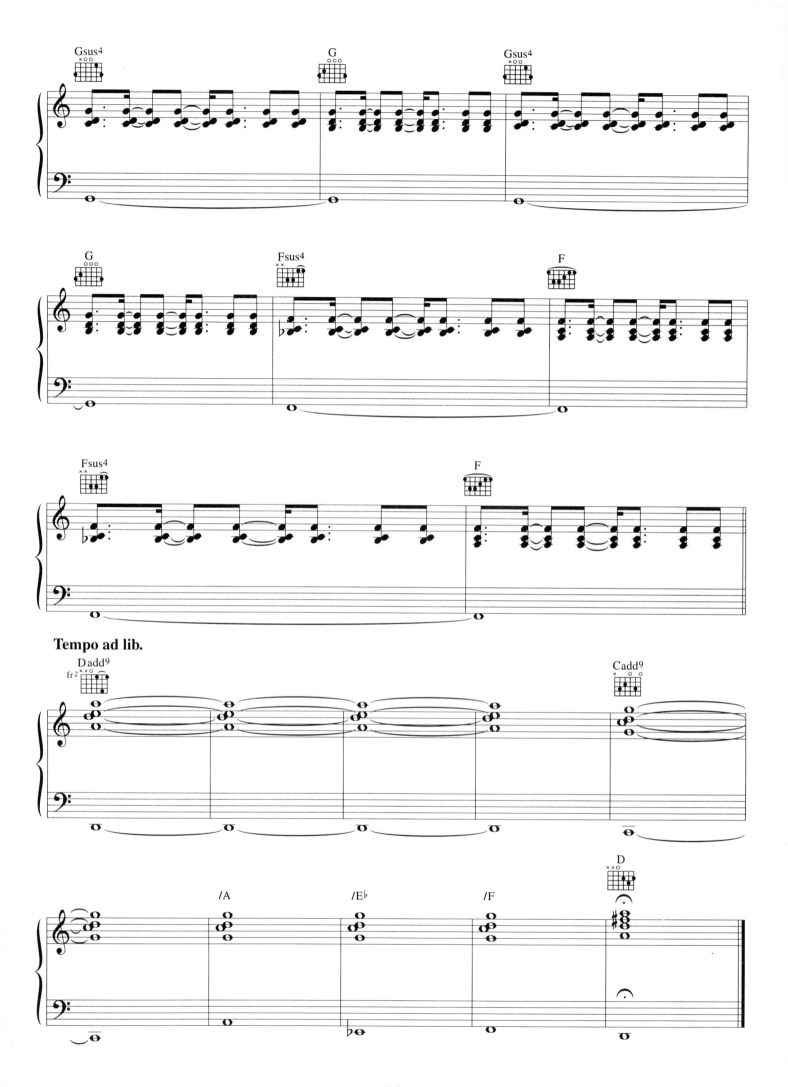

Tempo ad lib.

CAPTAIN WALKER

WORDS & MUSIC BY PETER TOWNSHEND

Cap - tain Wal - ker did - n't come home, his

un - born child will nev - er know him.
Be -

lieve him miss - ing with a num - ber of men, don't ex - pect to see him a - gain.

12

Cap - tain Wal - ker did - n't come home, Cap - tain Wal - ker did - n't come home,

Cap - tain Wal - ker did - n't come home, his un - born child will nev - er know

— him.

Segue

IT'S A BOY

WORDS & MUSIC BY PETER TOWNSHEND

TWENTY-ONE

WORDS & MUSIC BY PETER TOWNSHEND

some - how when you smile— I can brave bad wea - ther.

AMAZING JOURNEY

WORDS & MUSIC BY PETER TOWNSHEND

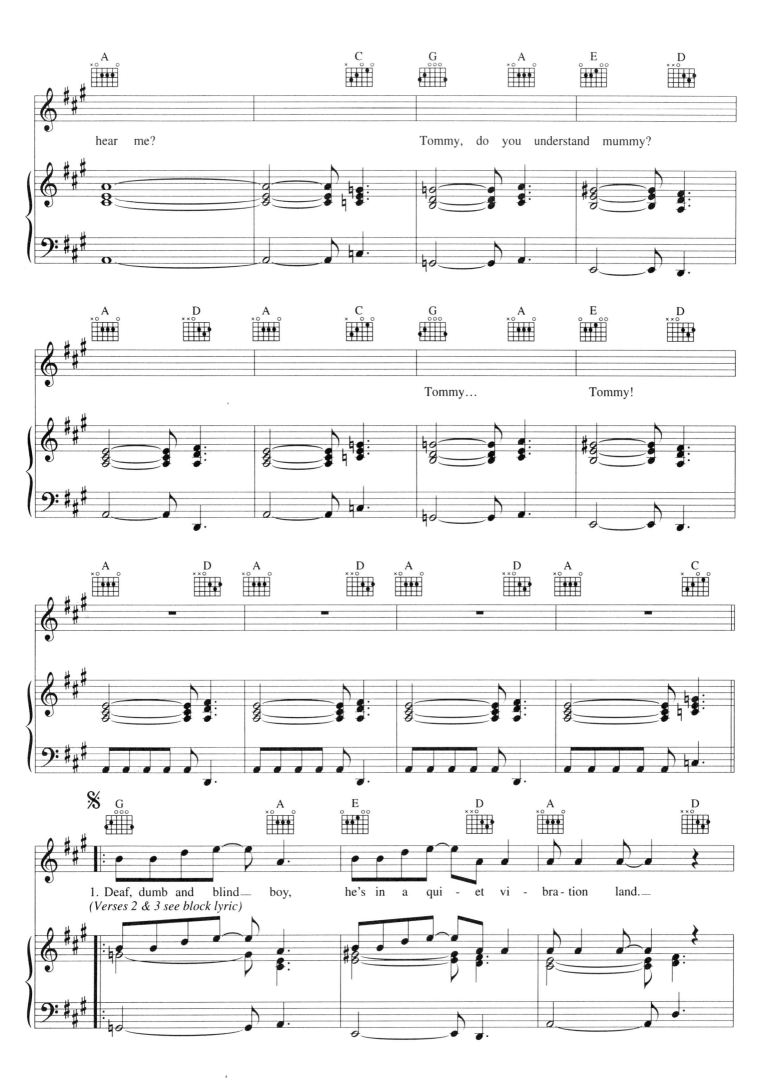

Strange as it seems,— his mu - si - cal dreams— ain't

quite so bad.

Sick - ness will sure - ly take—

i - ma - ges blind, I'll be your lead - er, I'll be your guide,— on the a -

To Coda ⊕

maz - ing jour - ney to - geth - er we'll— ride.

D.%. al Coda

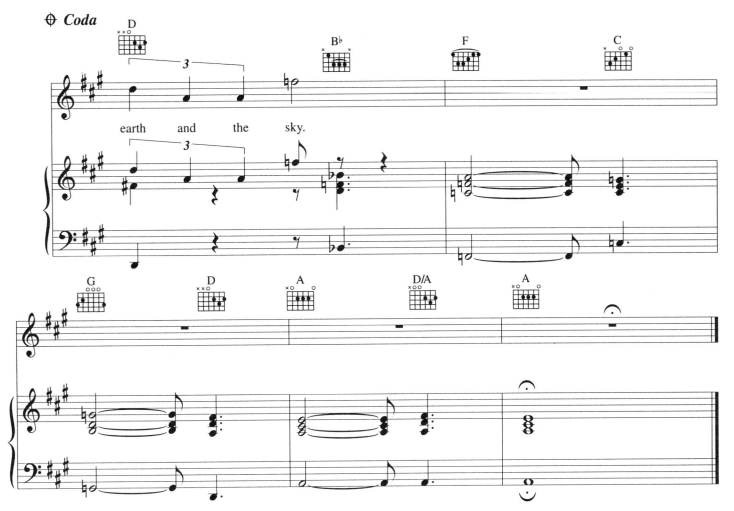

Verse 2:
Four years old
With thoughts as bold as thought can be
Loving life and becoming wise
In simplicity.

Verse 3:
Nothing to say
Nothing to hear
Nothing to see
Each sensation makes a note in his symphony.

Sickness will surely take the mind
Where minds can't usually go.
Come on the amazing journey
And learn all you should know.

His eyes are the eyes
That transmit all they know.
The truth burns so bright
It can melt winter snow.
A towering figure
So brilliant, so high
A white sun burning
The earth and the sky.

Additional lyric on reprise:
Ten years old
With thoughts as bold as thought can be
Loving life and becoming wise
In simplicity.

EYESIGHT TO THE BLIND

WORDS & MUSIC BY SONNY BOY WILLIAMSON

talk a-bout your wo-man, I wish you could see mine.
(Verses 2 & 3 see block lyric)

1. You

Verse 2:
You know her daddy gave her magic
I can tell by the way she walks.
Her daddy gave her magic
I can tell by the way she walks.
Every time she starts to shakin'
The dumb begin to talk.

Verse 3:
She's got the power to hear you
Never fear.
She's got the power to heal you
Never fear.
Just a word from her lips
And the deaf begin to hear.

CHRISTMAS/SEE ME, FEEL ME

WORDS & MUSIC BY PETER TOWNSHEND

(1. 3.) Did you ev-er see the fa-ces of the child-ren? They get so ex-cit-ed.
(Verse 2 see block lyric)

Wak-ing up on Christ-mas morn-ing, hours be-fore the win-ter sun's ig-

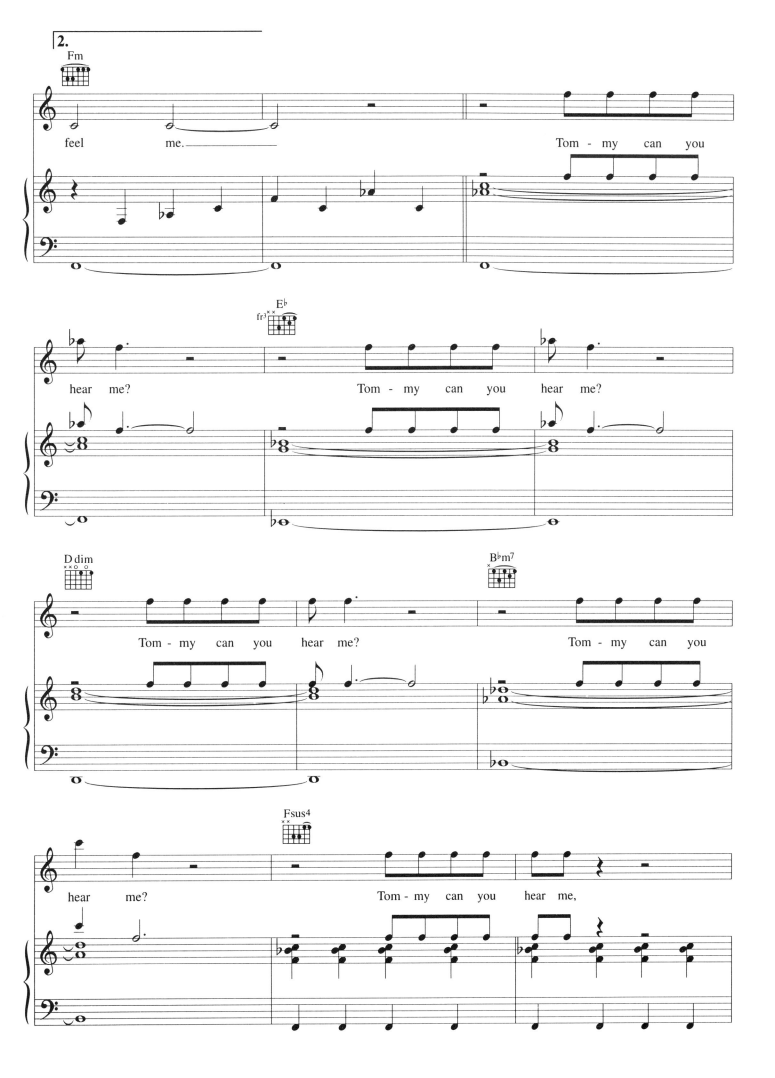

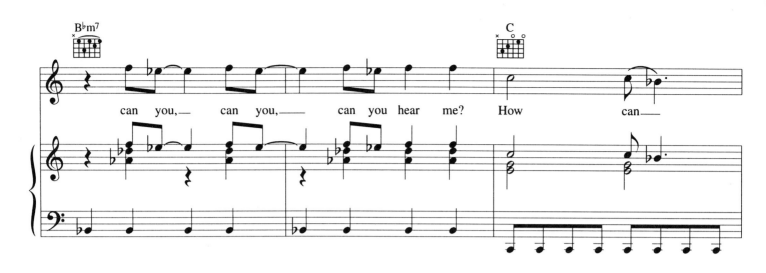

can you,— can you,— can you hear me? How can—

D.C. al Coda

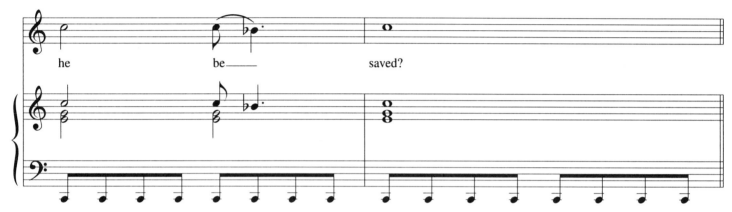

he be—— saved?

✵ *Coda*

Repeat to segue

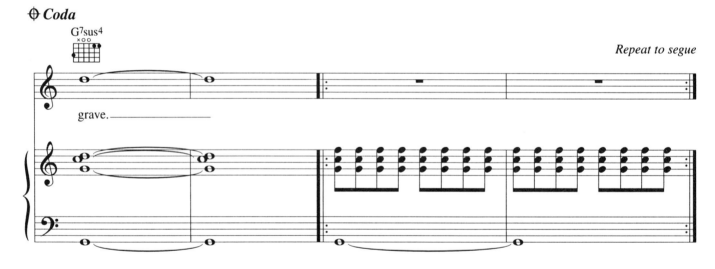

grave.—

Verse 2:
Surrounded by us all, he sits so silently
And unaware of anything.
Playing dumb, he cries, he smiles
He picks his nose, he pokes his tongue at everything.

I believe in love
But how can men who've never seen light be enlightened?
Only if he's cured
Will his spirit's future level ever heighten.

40

COUSIN KEVIN

WORDS & MUSIC BY JOHN ENTWISTLE

Lyrics:
1. We're on our own cou-sin, all a-lone cou-sin, let's think of a game to

Verse 2:
Maybe a cigarette burn on your arm
Would change your expression to one of alarm.
I'll drag you around by a lock of your hair
Or give you a push at the top of the stairs.

I'm the school bully,
The classroom cheat,
The nastiest play-friend
You ever could meet.
I'll put glass in your dinner
And spikes in your seat.

ACID QUEEN

WORDS & MUSIC BY PETER TOWNSHEND

road.

When the work is done, you'll look at him, he'll ne - ver be more a - live

my blood will run through his skin

watch his bo - dy writhe! I'm the

3. If your

D.%. al Coda

DO YOU THINK IT'S ALRIGHT

WORDS & MUSIC BY PETER TOWNSHEND

Do you think it's al - right _____
to leave the boy with Un - cle Er - - - - nie?

Do you think it's al - right _____

he's had a few too ma - - ny to -
Do you think it's al -

night.
right, I think it's al - right, yes I think it's al - -

right, do you think it's al - right?
right, yes I think it's al - right.

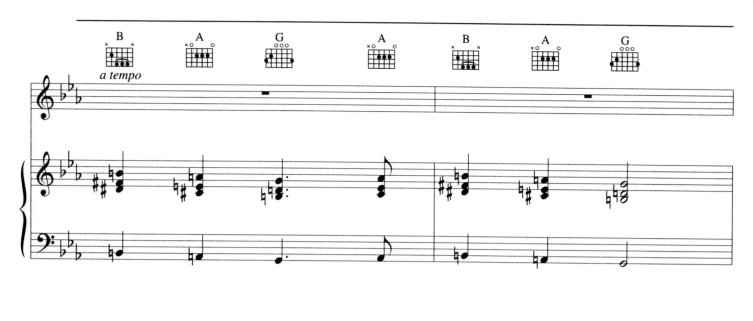

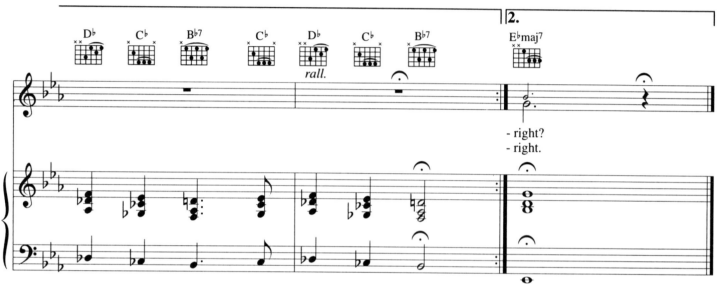

- right?
- right.

Verse 2:
Do you think it's alright
To leave the boy with Uncle Ernie?
Do you think it's alright,
There's something about this I don't really like.
 Do you think it's alright?
 I think it's alright
 Yes, I think it's alright
 Yes, I think it's alright
Do you think it's alright?
Yes, I think it's alright.

FIDDLE ABOUT

WORDS & MUSIC BY JOHN ENTWISTLE

I'm your wick-ed un-cle Er-nie, I'm glad you won't see or hear me as I fid-dle a-bout, fid-dle a-bout, fid-dle a-bout. Your mo-ther

left me here to mind you now I'm do-ing what I want to,

fid-dl-ing a-bout, fid-dl-ing a-bout, fid-dle a-bout.

Down with the bed clothes, up with the night shirt, fid-dle a-bout,

fid-dle a-bout, fid-dle a-bout.

Fid - dle a - bout, fid - dle a - bout,

fid - dle a - bout. You won't shout as I fid - dle a - bout.

play 3 times

Fid - dle a - bout, fid - dle a - bout, fid - dle a - bout.

accel. poco a poco   *play 6 times*

Fid - dle,_____ fid - dle,_____ fid - dle._____

59

THERE'S A DOCTOR

WORDS & MUSIC BY PETER TOWNSHEND

GO TO THE MIRROR/LISTENING TO YOU

WORDS & MUSIC BY PETER TOWNSHEND

GO TO THE MIRROR

1. He seems to be com-plete-ly un-re-cep-tive, the
(Verse 2 see block lyric)

tests I give him make no sense at all. His eyes re-act to light, the dials de-

tect it, he hears but can- not ans- wer to your call. ___

See me, feel me,

touch me, heal me. See me,

feel me, touch me, heal me. ___

LISTENING TO YOU

65

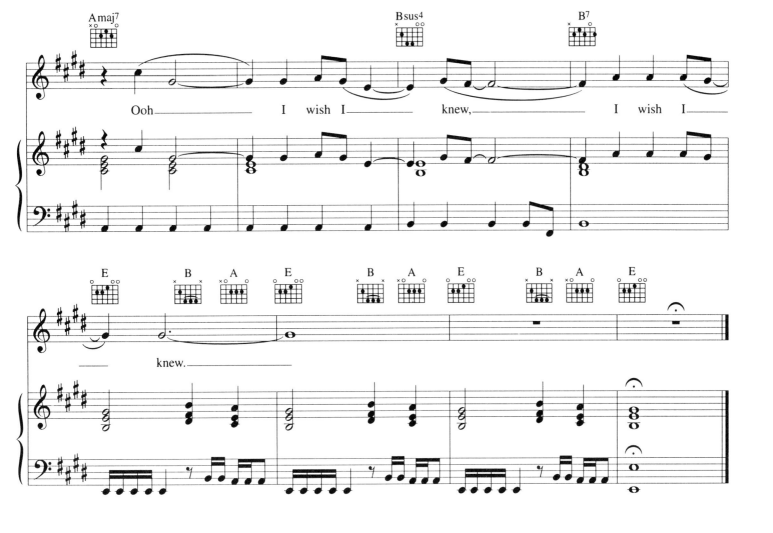

GO TO THE MIRROR

Verse 2:
There is no chance, no untried operation
All hope lies with him and none with me.
Imagine though, the shock from isolation
If he suddenly could hear and speak and see.

Verse 4:
I often wonder what he is feeling
Has he ever heard a word I've said?
Look at him in the mirror, dreaming
What is happening in his head?

LISTENING TO YOU

Verse 2:
Right behind you, I see the millions
On you, I see the glory
From you, I get opinions
From you, I get the story.

PINBALL WIZARD

WORDS & MUSIC BY PETER TOWNSHEND

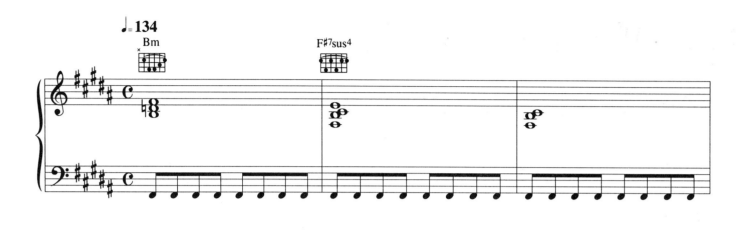

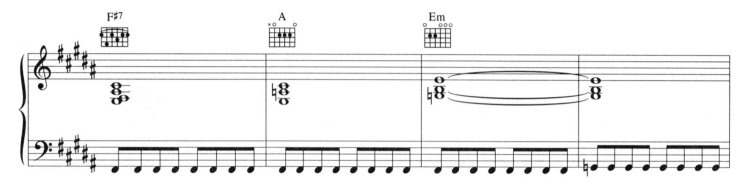

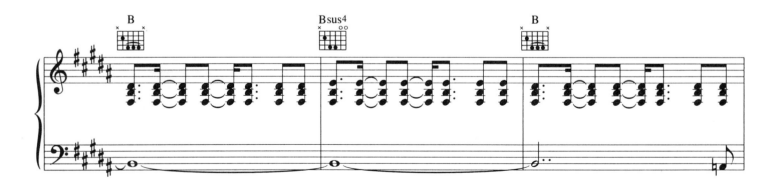

1. Ev - er since I was a young boy, I've

played the sil - ver ball,— from So - ho down to Brigh - ton, I

must have played them all.— But I ain't seen no - thing like him in

such a sup - ple wrist.

How do you think___ he does___ it?   I   don't___ know.

What makes him___ so   good?___   Ev- en

Ev- en

at my favour-ite ta-ble, he can beat my best, the kids all lead him in___ and

he just does the rest.___ He's got cra-zy flip-per fin - gers,

nev-er seen him fall, that deaf, dumb__ and blind__ kid, sure plays a mean pin -

ball.___

Verse 2:
He stands like a statue
Becomes part of the machine.
Feeling all the bumpers
Always playing clean.
He plays by intuition
The digit counters fall.
That deaf, dumb and blind kid
Sure plays a mean pinball.

Verse 3:
He's got no distractions
Can't hear those buzzers and bells.
Don't see no lights a' flashin'
He plays by sense of smell.
Always gets a replay
And never tilts at all.
That deaf, dumb and blind kid
Sure plays a mean pinball.

I thought I was
The Bally table king
But I just handed
My pinball crown to him.
How do you think he does it?
(I don't know)
What makes him so good?

Verse 4:
Even at my favourite table
He can beat my best
The kids all lead him in
And he just does the rest.
He's got crazy flipper fingers
Never seen him fall.
That deaf, dumb and blind kid
Sure plays a mean pinball.

TOMMY CAN YOU HEAR ME?

WORDS & MUSIC BY PETER TOWNSHEND

SMASH THE MIRROR

WORDS & MUSIC BY PETER TOWNSHEND

rise,   rise.   rise._____

Do you hear or fear, or   do I smash the mir - ror?_____

Do you hear or fear, or   do I smash the

mir - ror?_____

Do you hear or fear, or do I smash the mir - ror?

Do you hear or fear, or do I smash the mir - ror?

SENSATION
WORDS & MUSIC BY PETER TOWNSHEND

make your lungs— hold breath in - - side.
ha - zy - eyed,— they catch my glance.

Lov - ers break— ca - res - ses for— me,
Plea - sant shud - ders shake their sen - ses, my

love dis - tract - ed don't know why.
warm mo - men - tum throws their stance.

You'll

I'm___ a sen - sa - tion.___

3. I

leave a trail— of root - ed peo - ple, mes - me - rised— by

just the sight.

All these lov - ers feel me com - ing love as one,— in

MIRACLE CURE

WORDS & MUSIC BY PETER TOWNSHEND

Ex - tra, ex - tra, read all a - bout it, the
pin - ball wi - zard in a mi - ra - cle cure.
Ex - tra, ex - tra, read all a - bout it, ex - tra!

I'M FREE

WORDS & MUSIC BY PETER TOWNSHEND

I was wait-ing at the door, this place is sa-cred as a

tem - ple.

D.%. al Coda

I'm

⊕ *Coda*

95

SALLY SIMPSON

WORDS & MUSIC BY PETER TOWNSHEND

1. Out-side the house Mis-ter Simp-son an-noun-ces Sal-ly can't go to the meet-ing.— he goes on clean-ing his blue— Rolls Royce, and she runs in-side a' weep-ing.— She

gets to her room and cries___ on a pic-ture, al-ways keeps it by___ her.___ She

picks up a book of her fa-ther's life and throws it on___ the fire.___

To Coda ⊕

___ She knew from the start deep down in her heart___ that

she and Tom-my were worlds a-part___

99

spent all day do-in' up my hair, I've got-ta look ex-act-ly right.___

May-be he'll see that I___ can be free and I'll get back-stage___

___ to-night. She knew from the start deep down in her heart,___ that

she and Tom-my were worlds a-part.___

But her mo-ther said "Nev-er mind,— your part— is to

be what you'll be."

D.%. al Coda

(%) She

✛ *Coda*

The crowd goes cra-zy as

Tom-my hits the stage,— lit-tle Sal-ly is lost as the po-lice push— the crowd—

back in a rage.

A

flash of fire, the whole place stops, Tom-my is a tran-qui-li-ser,_____ but

Sal-ly's so hot, she risks a shot____ and jumps up on the ris-er._____ She's

up there now, she's hit the top,____ she brush-es his hand-some face.____

Tom-my whirls a-round as a u-ni-formed man ush-ers her from the stage.

She knew from the start deep down in her heart— that she and Tom-my were

104

Lyric on D.%.
She lands at six and the gig is a' rockin'
The devil is out tonight.
The band cuts loose and the stage is a' knockin'
But Sally just sits real tight.
She grabs her chair–she's hot to dance
Right down in the very front row.
Then a slick D.J. who is pissing his pants
Runs on and says: Here we go!

TOMMY'S HOLIDAY CAMP

WORDS & MUSIC BY KEITH MOON

Spoken: Hello my darlings!

I'm Tom-my's un-cle Er-nie and I wel-come you to Tom-my's Ho-li-day Camp. The

camp   with a   dif - fer - ence,   ne - ver mind— the   wea - ther,

when   you come   to   Tom - my's   the   ho - li - day is   for - ev – er.___

1.   2.   B♭   a tempo
rall.   //   //   //

2. Get   (Bless you, love!)

3.   //

camp   with a   dif - fer- ence,   ne - ver mind   the   wea-ther!

The

When you come to Tom-my's ———— the ho-li-day is for-ev-er. ————

rall.

Spoken: This is your chance. Tommy's holiday camp is coming to your town.
At eight tonight — Tommy, live on stage. You lucky people.

Verse 2:
Get your Tommy T-shirts and your stickers
And your Tommy mirrors to smash.
Don't rush… keep steady
Have your money ready
Buy your way to Heaven.
That comes to one pound seven.
Bless you, love!

Verse 3:
Buy your shades and ear-plugs here
Keep in line, I've got a huge supply.
Get your Tommy record
You can really hear him talk.
Tommy pics and badges
Half a nicker for the cork.
Watch this then!

WELCOME

WORDS & MUSIC BY PETER TOWNSHEND

get them all in. Come to this house, _____

in - to this house! _____

ple.

Lo - ve - ly bright home,

danc - ing all night, nev - er sleep - ing.

There's more at the door, there's

more at the door, there's more at the door, there's more at the door, there's

more at the door, there's more at the door, there's more at the door, there's

more. We need more room, build an ex-ten-sion, we'll

all work to-geth-er, spare no ex-pense now. Come to this house,

be one of us,

come in to this house, be one of us.

Come to our house,

come to me now.

WE'RE NOT GOING TO TAKE IT

WORDS & MUSIC BY PETER TOWNSHEND

not, I hope— that's clear— you should-n't try to ape my show,— it is-n't just— pin-ball— you don't need to claim a share of my pain, you're nor — mal af - - ter all.

sake you. May - be rape you, let's for - get you, bet - ter

still.

123

Verse 2:

You don't need to hear me,
You've got ideas of your own.
Don't have to come and cheer me,
That's something you've outgrown.
You don't need to see me,
Your vision makes the scene.
Don't let Uncle Ernie make you play
On Tommy's old machine!